TROLL JOKES AND RIDDLES

by Linda Longo

illustrated by Dan Nevins

Watermill Press

Library of Congress Cataloging-in-Publication Data
Longo, Linda, (date)
    Troll jokes & riddles / by Linda Longo.
        p.   cm.
    Summary: A collection of jokes and riddles featuring trolls, such
as "What do trolls say when they first meet? Small world, isn't it?"
    ISBN 0-8167-2940-9
1. Trolls—Juvenile humor.   2. Riddles, Juvenile.   3. American wit
and humor.   [1. Trolls—Wit and humor.   2. Riddles.   3. Jokes.]
I. Title.   II. Title: Troll jokes and riddles.
PN6231.T73L66   1993
818'.5402—dc20   92-22571

Printed in the United States of America.
10 9 8 7 6 5 4 3 2 1

What kind of troll shaves 25 times a day?

A barber troll.

Why did the silly troll put his head down on the piano keys?

He was trying to play by ear.

What did the troll do when he broke his toe?

He called a troll truck.

Why did the silly troll plant light bulbs?

He wanted to grow street lights.

What happened to the blue troll when he jumped into the Black Sea?

He got wet.

**How did Tommy Troll build up his
flea-collar business?**

He started from scratch.

What do you call a 2,000-pound troll?

"Sir."

How do trolls send messages to each other?

They send a *troll*agram.

What do trolls say when they first meet?

"Small world, isn't it?"

What kind of assignment do trolls bring home from school?

*Gnome*work.

Which month do trolls talk the least?

February. It's the shortest month.

Why did the silly troll take a hammer to bed?

He wanted to hit the sack.

How did the troll get to work?

He took the *troll*ey.

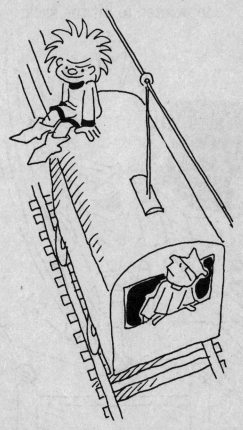

Do trolls write with their left or their right hands?

Neither. They write with pens.

What does a troll call his house?

Gnome Sweet Gnome.

Why couldn't the egg lend the troll any money?

It was broke.

**What kind of song did the troll sing
in the car?**

A car-tune.

**Why do we dress little girl trolls in pink
and little boy trolls in blue?**

Because they can't dress themselves.

Why did the troll farmer call a doctor?

His corn had an earache.

What do you call a troll who sells tires?

A wheel-estate dealer.

Why was the troll's house full of rabbits?

He had central hare conditioning.

How many sandwiches can a troll eat on an empty stomach?

One. After he eats the first one, his stomach is no longer empty.

What do you call a troll with cotton in his ears?

Anything you want. He can't hear you.

How can you get a troll to fly?

Buy him an airline ticket.

What kind of car do rich trolls drive?

A *Trolls*-Royce.

Why did the troll reporter go to the ice-cream store?

He needed a scoop.

**What do you call a troll who operates
an armored car?**

A safe driver.

**Why did the silly troll parents keep their
son in the refrigerator?**

So he wouldn't get spoiled.

What do you say when you meet a two-headed troll?

"Hello, hello."

What happened when the troll went to dinner with a bottle of glue?

He got stuck with the bill.

What makes more noise than a troll singing as loudly as he can?

Two trolls singing.

What is the tallest building in Troll Village?

The library. It has the most stories.

Why did Timmy Troll put on a wet shirt and pants?

The label said "Wash and Wear."

**Ten trolls were walking under one tiny
umbrella but none of them got wet.
Why not?**

It wasn't raining.

Why did Tina Troll throw the clock out the window?

She wanted to see time fly.

What happened when the troll received a huge electric bill?

He was shocked.

Why did the troll become a baker?

He kneaded the dough.

Why did Mr. and Mrs. Troll name their daughter Sugar?

Because she was so refined.

Why did the student troll take a parachute to school?

In case he had to drop out.

What did Tabitha Troll do when her puppy chewed up her spelling book?

She took the words right out of his mouth.

What kind of candy do little trolls eat?

*Troll*ipops.

Why couldn't the troll cross the bridge?

He didn't have money for the *troll*booth.

Why did the troll farmer plant old car parts in his garden?

He wanted to grow a bumper crop.

When does a troll weigh as much as an elephant?

When the scale is broken.

Why did Tommy Troll take his bike to school?

He wanted to drive his teacher up the wall.

What happened when the teenage troll ate 12 hot dogs?

He was sick with puppy love.

How can a troll double his money right away?

By folding it in half.

What happened when the troll ate a roll of film?

The doctor told him nothing serious would develop.

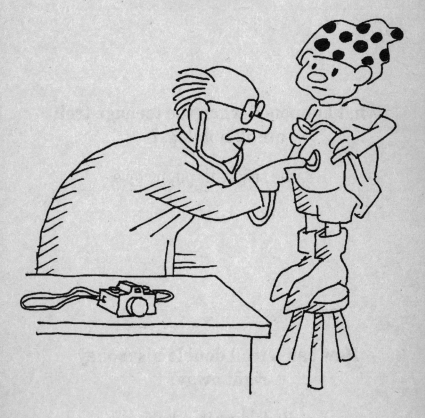

Why did the troll go to bed with a yardstick?

He wanted to see how long he would sleep.

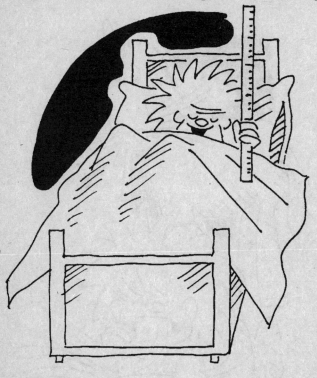

What happened to the troll who fell on a record player?

He got a slipped disc.

Why did the young troll eat hay for dinner?

His parents said he eats like a horse.

Why did the troll want to work in a mattress factory?

So he could lie down on the job.

Why did the silly troll buy a set of tools?

His teacher said he had a screw loose.

Why did the silly troll cut a hole in the top of his umbrella?

He wanted to know if it had stopped raining.

Why did Tina Troll put sugar under her pillow?

She wanted to have sweet dreams.

What did the little troll say to the lollipop?

"I can lick you any day."

Why did Tabitha Troll want to work for the watch factory?

So she could make faces all day.

Why did the troll's dog jump into the river?

He wanted to chase catfish.

What happened when Granny Troll bought some steel wool?

She knitted a very scratchy sweater.

Why did the silly troll think he was good in sports?

Because he had athlete's foot.

Why did the silly troll eat dinner at the duck pond?

He wanted to have quackers with his soup.

Why did the troll wear loud socks?

To keep his feet from falling asleep.

Why is a baby troll like an old car?

They both have a rattle.

RATTLE RATTLE

Why is it so hard to borrow money from trolls?

Because they're always short.

Why did the troll bus driver go broke?

Because he drove all his customers away.

Why did the bald troll buy a rabbit farm?

Because he wanted to grow some hares.

Why are trolls so healthy?

They drink a lot of well water.

How did the silly troll bump his head raking leaves?

He fell out of the tree.

Why did Timmy Troll put a clock under his desk?

He wanted to work overtime.

What happened to the troll who covered herself with vanishing cream?

Nobody knows.

How do you know when there's a large troll in your refrigerator?

The door won't close.

Why did Mr. Troll wear a bathing suit to work?

He rode to the office in a car-pool.

When five trolls fell into the water, how come only four got their hair wet?

One of them was bald.

What happens when Granny Troll gets out of her chair?

She goes off her rocker.

Why did the troll farmer take a bale of hay to bed with him?

To feed his nightmare.

Why did the silly troll stand on a ladder when he sang a song?

He wanted to reach the high notes.

**Why did the teenage troll hold a stone
and a hot-dog bun up to her ears?**

She wanted to hear rock and roll.

**Why was Tommy Troll afraid to walk
on the marble floor?**

He thought it would roll away.

Why did the troll throw a bucket of water off the roof?

She wanted to make a big splash.